# SPOOL
# KNITTING

BY
## MARY A. McCORMACK

1909

# CONTENTS

|  | PAGE |
|---|---|
| Spool Knitting | 1 |
| Toy Knitters. | 3 |
| Round Web | 5 |
| Flat Web | 7 |
| Circular Mat | 9 |
| Ball for Baby | 11 |
| Doll's Muff | 13 |
| Collarette. | 15 |
| Tom O'Shanter Cap | 17 |
| Baby's Rattle | 19 |
| Toboggan Cap | 21 |
| Child's Bath or Bedroom Slippers | 23 |
| Small Mittens. | 25 |
| Doll's Hood | 27 |
| Doll's Coat or Jacket | 29 |
| Bootees | 33 |
| Little Boy Blue | 35 |
| Little Red Riding Hood | 37 |
| Doll's Skirt | 39 |
| Little Boy's Hat | 41 |
| Child's Muffler | 43 |
| Child's Hood | 45 |
| Little Girl's Hat | 47 |
| Doll's Sweater | 49 |
| Wristlets | 51 |
| Shoulder Shawl | 53 |
| Doll's Carriage Robe | 55 |
| Child's Leggings | 57 |
| Muffler | 59 |
| Made of Knitting Cotton | 61 |
| Jumping Rope | 63 |
| Toy Horse Reins | 65 |
| Wash Cloth | 67 |
| School Bag | 69 |
| Chimney Cleaner | 71 |
| Doll's Hammock | 73 |

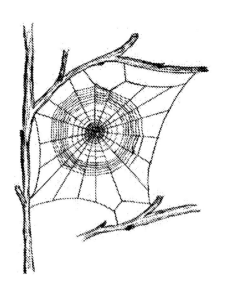

# SPOOL KNITTING

Few elementary exercises have aroused more interest in the child than the toy knitting; due, perhaps, to its simplicity and his power to do it easily and well.

To some keen observer the little orb-weaving spider may have suggested this form of occupation. Be this as it may, the child who is a lover of nature will be quick to perceive the strong resemblance he bears to this little insect while at work with his toy knitter, going from post to post just as the insect worked its net in spiral form on his framework of radiating lines.

The possibilities of an empty spool and a few pins are almost without limitations. The illustrations here given are merely suggestive of many more that can be worked out along these lines. They are not simply to momentarily attract the child, but to permit of individual growth, and to have him participate in the joy of its ultimate use.

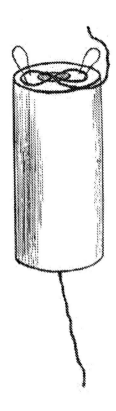

## Toy Knitters

Toy knitters are made of a cylindrical piece of wood two and one-half or three inches long and at least one inch in diameter. This size enables the child to grasp it easily and work without cramping the fingers. A hole one-fourth or one-half inch in diameter is bored lengthwise through the center to admit the work. Spools are used to advantage where knitters cannot be obtained.

Pins, staples, or wire nails are used as posts. These are driven into the wood and then curved outward a little at the top with pliers, to prevent the work from slipping off. One, two, three or four posts may be used.

A number of forms of web can be made, but the simplest and quickest are those made on the knitters having but two posts. The four-post knitters are also simple and are used where a thick cord is needed.

Except otherwise specified two-post knitters are used for these models.

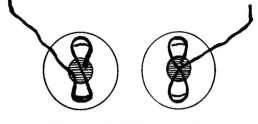

## Round Web

Drop worsted through the hole in the center of the knitter and draw it out at the other end, three inches. This end is used to draw the work through the knitter. Carry the worsted leading from the ball, around the post to the right, across the center of the hole in the knitter and around the post to the left ; then back across the center to the post at the right, thus making two stitches on this post. Lift the lower or first stitch with a large pin or knitting needle, carry it over the second stitch and drop it over the post ; then across the center to the post at the left and repeat. So continue until the desired length is obtained.

It will require seven yards of yarn to make one yard of web on the two-post knitter.

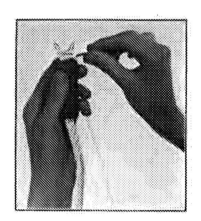

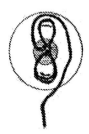

## Flat Web

Begin in the same way as for round web, but after carrying the first or lower stitch over the second stitch on each post, bring the worsted back around the same post, and over to the post on the opposite side and repeat. This will leave two stitches on each post. In knitting flat webs, two stitches must always be left on the end posts, and these two are carried over the third stitch and dropped over the post in working back and forth.

It requires eleven yards of yarn to make one yard of flat web on the two-post knitter.

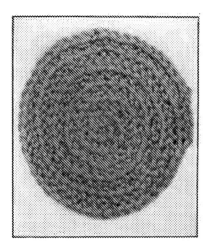

## Circular Mat

A mat five inches in diameter requires two and one-half yards of round web. Start sewing with the piece of worsted hanging from the end of the web. Coil and sew in place by taking up the underhalf of a stitch on the right, then the underhalf of a stitch on the left side usually called "ball stitch." Continue alternating from right to left, taking up one stitch at a time except when it is necessary to widen; then sew two stitches of the web into one in the mat.

Run the end of sewing thread back in the sewing to fasten it. When starting with a new sewing thread, put the needle in one inch back from where sewing ended and run it through the work to where the last stitch was taken.

## Ball for Baby

Use round web. Start with end of web and sew and coil as for round mat. Widen only when necessary to keep it from drawing in too quickly. When desired width or center of ball is reached, fill with tissue paper or a ball of soft cotton. The sewing is then continued and each row narrowed off by taking two stitches in part already sewed and one in the web. When the same number of rows is narrowed the filling should be entirely covered. The end left over will serve as a cord for the ball.

Flat web may be used by taking twelve pieces three inches long and sewing them together—alternating color and white, if desired. Run a draw-thread around the bottom and fill with paper or cotton; then run a draw-thread around the top. Finish with a cord made of a piece of round web.

## Doll's Muff

This will require three yards of round web. Sew the web into a rectangular piece three inches wide and five inches long.

Join the three-inch ends together and draw up the ends a little to form the muff. Finish with cord to go around the neck.

## Collarette

Round web five yards. Measure the doll's
neck for collar. Gradually widen each row in
the back. Bring the third row of web down in
front to form the tabs; then up to the back
of collarette and finish the back, bringing the
last row down in front into the tabs.

Paper patterns may be used as a guide, but
children should be encouraged to draw and cut
their own patterns.

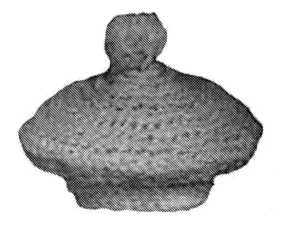

## Tam O' Shanter Cap

Measure the doll's head and make the top of the crown twice the diameter of the head. It is sewed in the same way as the circular mat. When the desired width of crown is obtained, begin the under side of the crown by narrowing off—that is, taking two stitches in the crown and sewing them into one stitch in the web. Continue until the desired opening for the head is obtained. Two rows of web will complete the headband. Finish with a pompon on top.

Use round web.

## Baby's Rattle

The foundation ring is made of a piece of splint or flat pith fifteen inches long. Form this into a ring, having the ends lap two inches. Wrap this with knitting cotton or yarn, being careful to keep winding even. When the winding is completed, draw the end of cotton underneath the winding with a needle to fasten it.

Use three pieces of round web for spokes. Fasten all three together in the center. Bells may be sewed on the outside or inside of the ring.

## Toboggan Cap

To make a cap five inches long and four inches wide, knit eighty-four inches of flat web. Begin five inches from the end of the web, turn and sew into a rectangular form five inches wide and eight inches long.

Join the five-inch ends, and draw in the top with the needle and a piece of the material from which the cap was made. After securing the top, twist and fold the piece of yarn remaining for a cord and fasten a number of strands of yarn through the loop for a tassel.

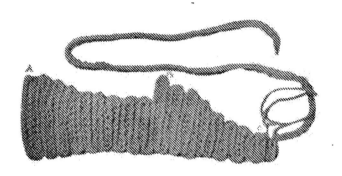

## Child's Bath or Bedroom Slippers

Length of sole, five and one-half inches. It is well to have the soles before beginning to sew. They can be secured at any store.

Each slipper requires two and one-half yards of round web. Start at the back of the heel (A, of illustration), and make the first two rows three inches high, then gradually shorten the next three rows, and keep each row this height until the instep is finished. The first row on the vamp (B, of illustration) is made one inch higher than the side. Each row is then gradually shortened, the last row being three-fourths of an inch high (C, of illustration). This will complete one-half of the slipper.

The other half is made in just the reverse way by continuing the sewing from the toe (C, of illustration) back to the heel, taking care that each row is exactly the same height as the corresponding row on the opposite side.

Join the back of the heel and sew to the soles before closing the vamp in front. Sew vamp up the center by catching corresponding loops together. Make cord and tassel to go around the top, as in illustration of finished slippers.

## Small Mittens

Sixty inches of flat web will be required for each mitten. Cut off eight pieces six inches long. In cutting, clip just one stitch and run the ends across, and sew them into a cylindrical form. Draw in the top with a needle and a piece of the material and fasten securely. Leave an opening on one side for the thumb.

The thumb is made of three pieces sewed together. The longest piece is three inches and the others each two and three-fourths inches long. In sewing it into the mitten, have the longest piece come down toward the wrist. Gradually form and sew it in place. Draw in the top and fasten securely.

### CORD

This is made of round web, knitted the desired length. The length will vary a little according to size of the child, but four and one-half feet is a good length. The mittens are fastened to the ends of the cord.

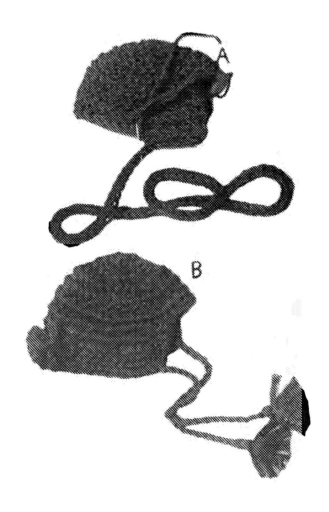

## Doll's Hood

This requires two yards of round web.

Start with the end of the web and sew into a circular form for the crown. (See illustration A.) The sixth row is brought down to within one inch of the center of the back. Turn and sew around to within one inch from the center of the back on the opposite side. This will leave two inches free in the back of the hood. Turn and continue sewing in this way for five rows, which will form the side of hood.

The remaining part of the web is then brought around the face of the hood and across the back, as one would sew a cord.

Finish with cord and tassel for tie-strings. A rosette of yarn may be made for the top or side.

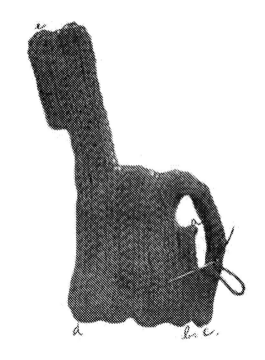

## Doll's Coat or Jacket

This may be made of round or flat web.

The coat is begun at the under-arm seam *a*.
For a coat five inches long begin three inches
from the end of the web to make the first turn.
Sew from this turn to the starting end of the
web *b*, fasten the sewing thread and cut it off.
The second row is made eleven inches long, or
long enough to go over the shoulder and down
the back, *b* to *c*.

Sew four rows in this way to form the front
and part of the back; then four rows five inches
long for the back; then four more rows eleven
inches long for the other shoulder and front *d*
to *e*. Sew the fifth or last row up three inches
for the other under-arm seam.

Join the under-arm seams, leaving an opening
of two inches for sleeves if they are desired. If
not, the armhole and neck can be finished off
with some contrasting color.

For the sleeves, measure the length of the
doll's arm and make the first row this length.
Make each row a little longer than the preceding row until the top or shoulder part is reached,
then gradually shorten each row until the desired
width is obtained. The last row should be the

same length as the first row. When sewing them in the coat, have the longest part come at the top of the shoulder. Buttons are made by braiding yarn and sewing it in the form of buttons.

A cord for fastening is made by braiding, or twisting and folding the yarn. It is then sewed into loops or used as cord and tassel for tying.

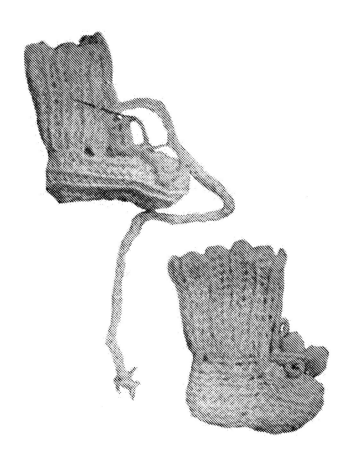

## Bootees

Knit two yards of round web for each bootee.
Start two inches from the end of the web for
the first turn. Sew into an elliptical form three
and one-half inches long for the sole. Sew two
more rows without widening for the sides of the
foot; then sew two rows across the front for the
toe; the third row bring all around the top to
complete the foot.

The leg of the bootee is made by bringing the
web directly upward three inches before making
the first turn. Make each row three inches high
and catch each row into the top of the foot
while sewing. Put cord and tassel around
where the leg and foot meet.

## Little Boy Blue

Make coat according to directions given for doll's coat.

Measure the length of the doll's leg for the length of the trousers. Use flat web and sew it into two rectangular pieces wide enough to make each leg a little full.

Join the inside seams part way and then join the open edge of the right front with the open edge of the left front. Do the same with the back edges. Put a draw-string around the top, or a piece of the web may be used for a waist-band. Put in a draw-string around the bottom of each leg.

## Little Red Riding-Hood

The doll shown in illustration is ten and one-half inches tall. To make cape and hood in one piece sew two rows of flat web, six and one-half inches long, for the center of the back. These two rows will also give the desired fulness. The next five rows are made nineteen inches long, or long enough to reach over the head and down to form the two sides of the cape and hood. After these five rows are completed, sew five rows six inches long on each side of the front of the cape, to make it wide enough to meet across the chest.

Close the cape and the hood in the back. The part above the six and a half inch rows will form the hood. Draw in the top of these two short rows and sew to the base of the hood. Put in a draw-string around the top of the right side of the cape in front, carry it around the base of the hood, around the top of the cape on the left side and tie in front.

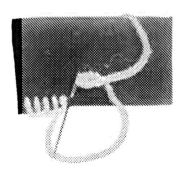

## Doll's Skirt

This skirt is five inches long and made of flat web. The first and last rows are made one and a quarter inch shorter than the other rows forming the skirt. These two rows are sewed together when the skirt is finished, thus forming the placket and also the desired fulness in the back.

There are sixteen rows in all. Each two, when sewed together, form a scollop at the top and bottom where the web is turned. In sewing care must be taken to have each row the exact length of the preceding row except in the first and last row.

The top of the skirt may be finished with a draw-string or a band made from cloth. The bottom of the skirt may be left as it is, or be finished with a blanket stitch of some contrasting color. The skirt requires five yards of flat web.

## Little Boy's Hat

Measure the child's head for the size of the hat. Make the crown of the hat one-half of this measurement. If the child's head measures twenty-two inches around, make the crown eleven inches in diameter. The crown is circular and is made in the same way as the circular mat, taking two stitches of web and sewing them into one stitch of the crown already sewed to keep it flat. When it is of the desired size, begin the side by sewing one stitch of the web into one of the crown, at the same time holding the web to be sewed directly under the last row in the crown.

Make the side twice as long as the desired height of the hat. For instance, if the desired height is to be three and a half inches, make the side seven inches long, as one-half of this measurement is turned up.

Two colors may be used, one color for the crown and one for the side. Red and black or red and white are pretty combinations.

A doll's hat of the same style, the crown three and a half inches in diameter, requires five yards of round web.

## Child's Muffler

This is a combination of flat and round web. Knit ten inches of flat web, change to round web by bringing the yarn across the center of the hole in the knitter to the opposite post, and knit ten inches, or the number of inches necessary to go around the neck. Change again to flat web, knit ten inches and clip off.

Make seven such pieces and sew them together to form the muffler. The round web will form the neck part.

Do not remove from the knitter while changing from flat to round web.

## Child's Hood

This is made much in the same way as the doll's hood. Make the back of the hood five inches in diameter, then turn the web and form the side. Sew around to within four inches of the place of turning on the opposite side and turn again. So continue until the side is sufficiently wide to cover the child's head. Extend this side three inches beyond the desired width, widening on each row of the extended part to give fulness. This widening may be omitted, and the extended part turned back, leaving it perfectly plain, if desired. Trim with rosettes or pompons made of the same material as the hood.

Turn back the extended part and tack to the hood. Sew a pompon or a rosette of yarn over the top of the sewing stitch. For tie-strings, use cord and tassel, or ribbon.

The hood requires from twenty-five to thirty yards.

## Little Girl's Hat

This requires twenty-five yards of round web. Measure the child's head for the size of the hat. Start the crown in the same way as the circular mat. When it is five inches in diameter, gradually turn the crown, while sewing the next five or six rows.

When the desired width is reached, begin forming the side by sewing one stitch of web into one stitch of the crown, keeping each row exactly under the preceding row until the desired height is obtained; then gradually widen to form the rim, which is three and a half or four inches broad.

Do not widen any on the last two rows, but draw the web a little tighter while sewing to make the edge of the rim roll or turn inward.

Finish with cord and tassels around the crown, or pompons on the right or left side of the front of the hat.

## Doll's Sweater

This is made of five and one-half yards of flat web cut into pieces of a desired length. Cut three pieces seven inches long for the front. One inch and a half of this will also form the neck. When cutting, clip only one stitch and pull out the ends.

The next two pieces are cut five and one-half inches long and sewed one on each side of the front one inch and a half below the top end. Each succeeding row is made a little shorter to form the shoulder, the shortest pieces forming the outside edges.

Make the back of the sweater in the same way and sew front and back together, leaving one and a quarter inch opening on each side for the sleeves.

The sleeve is made of five pieces, the longest piece being three inches, and the shortest two and one-half inches long. Sew these pieces together to form the sleeve. When sewing it into the sweater, place the longest part at the shoulder seam and stretch the armhole while sewing it in.

## Wristlets

These are made of round or flat web. Each wristlet requires one and one-half yards.

Measure five inches, the length of the wrist-let, and turn. Start sewing from this point and sew to the end of the five inches and turn again.

Continue until enough rows are sewed to make the wristlet the desired width, which in this model is two and one-half inches.

## Shoulder Shawl

This may be made of round or flat web, and of any desired size. If the shawl is to be thirty-six inches long, clip the web into pieces of this length and sew them together until the shawl is of the desired width, or the web may simply be turned at the end of each row, then proceed with the sewing.

The fringe for the ends is made by cutting the yarn into lengths twice as long as the desired length of the fringe—that is, if the fringe is to be five inches long, cut the yarn into pieces ten inches long.

Fold each ten-inch piece in two, slip the folded end through a stitch in the end of the shawl and draw the two ends of the piece through the loop thus formed and pull tight.

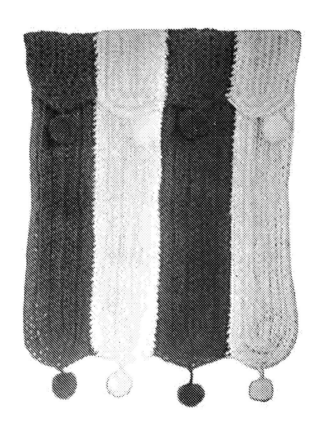

## Doll's Carriage Robe

This robe is ten inches wide and eighteen inches long, and is made of four pieces of flat web, each piece three yards long. Any number of pieces of either round or flat web may be used, and the robe made wider and longer if desired.

Measure fifteen inches of web and turn it. Begin sewing from this, turn down to the end of the fifteen inches and again turn, bringing the web around over the end. Care must be taken while turning to keep the ends perfectly flat.

When the three yards are used begin the other parts in the same way. Make four or any desired number of parts, and sew them together, alternating the colors. Put a tassel made of the same material on the rounded end of each part.

If round web is used it will require more for each part, for the round is not as wide as the flat web.

## Child's Leggings

Leggings may be made of round or flat web. Measure five inches above the knee down to the vamp of the shoe for the length of the front part of the legging. This gives the length of the first row.

Turn the web and begin to sew from this point up to the top, then turn again and sew down to the toe. Continue in this way until the front part is two and one-half inches wide.

Bring the remaining rows down to within two inches of the end of the toe, until the legging is wide enough to go around the child's leg, then sew to the opposite side of the front. Sew a piece of tape to the instep.

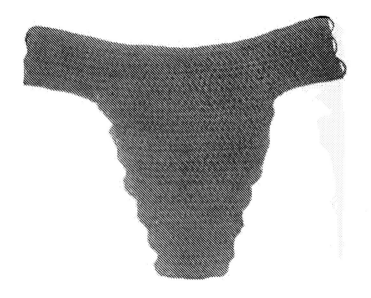

## Muffler

This may be made of round or flat web. Make the part to go around the neck first. In this model the neck band is ten inches long and three inches wide. Sew four rows of flat or six rows of round web for the neck. Begin three inches from the ends to make the front. Gradually shorten each row until it is of the desired length.

Make loops of twisted yarn and sew to one end of the neck band to slip over the buttons. Sew the buttons on the opposite end and on the inside where they will be hidden while the muffler is being worn.

## Made of Knitting Cotton

Knitting cotton can be secured at any department store. It comes in colors white, black, red, navy blue, and mixed colors. This is not as elastic as worsted and is used where strength is required, such as bags, hammocks, wash-cloths, etc. It is very inexpensive and can be used to great advantage.

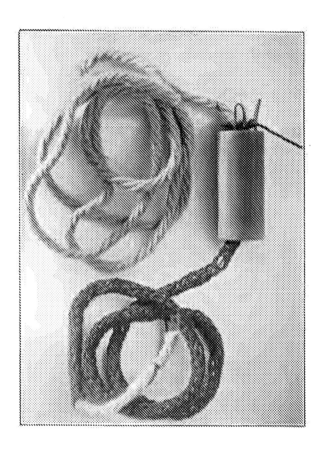

## Jumping Rope

Select a piece of jute, or stout cord the length of the desired rope.   Drop one end of this and one end of the knitting cotton through the hole in the knitter (use knitter having four posts), and draw it out at the other end three inches.   Bring the cotton leading from the ball around each post once, then proceed with the knitting, covering the cord or jute which is used as a core or foundation for the rope.

Cords for pillow tops may also be made in this way.

## Toy Horse Reins

These are made of coarse knitting cotton on four-post knitters. Knit a piece three yards long for the reins. The children measure each other for the breast-piece, which will be from ten to twelve inches long. This is fastened to the reins nine inches below the center of the neck on each side, to allow the head to pass through easily.

Two colors may be used in knitting the reins, working around first with one color, then with the other.

Fourteen yards of knitting cotton will make one yard of web on the four-post knitter.

## Wash Cloth

This is made of white knitting cotton. It requires nine yards of web for a cloth ten by twelve inches. Measure twelve inches of web, turn and sew toward the end.

When the twelve-inch piece is sewed turn again and sew. Continue in this way until the desired size is obtained.

With a piece of the cotton make a loop at one corner by which to hang it.

## School Bag

This may be made of round or flat web. A bag twelve inches deep and fourteen inches wide requires thirty yards. Measure twenty-four inches of web and turn. Begin sewing from this turn to the end of the twenty-four inches then turn again. So continue until this oblong piece measures fourteen by twenty-four inches. Fold this in two and sew up the sides. This will avoid any seam in the bottom of the bag.

Make handles in the same way as for jumping-rope, or a double thickness of the web may be used for each handle and sewed to the top sides of the bag. Finish by sewing a piece of the web around the top.

Laundry bags, sewing bags, and little bags for holding paints and water-dish may be made in similar way.

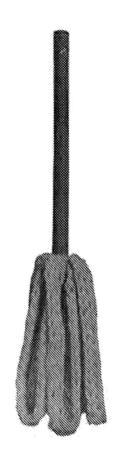

## Chimney Cleaner

This is made of white knitting cotton. It requires two yards of flat or three yards of round web.

Secure a piece of stick or better still a piece of half-inch dowel ten or twelve inches long, for a handle. Cut a groove with a knife around one end to keep the web from slipping off.

Sew the web into loops three and a half or four inches long. Draw them in around the end of the handle with the sewing string just in the groove; then wind the sewing string around two or three times, tie, and clip off the ends.

## Doll's Hammock

This is made of flat web.  A hammock eight by twelve inches requires five and one-half yards.  Sew this into an oblong piece twelve inches long and eight inches wide.

Secure a piece of cardboard three inches longer than the oblong piece and one inch wider.

Round off the corners with a pair of scissors (see illustration), and cut notches or slits in ends one-half inch apart.  Sew two brass rings in the center of one side, and on the other baste the oblong piece which is to be used for the hammock.  Then with a needle and a long piece of the knitting cotton begin making the ends of the hammock by securing one end of the sewing string to the hammock and bring it over the end of the cardboard in the first slit from the end and through the ring on the opposite side of cardboard; back over cardboard, through second slit and through hammock.

So continue until one end is finished.  Do the same with the other end.  These strings may be held in place by putting three or four rows of weaving just underneath the rings.

Clip the basting stitches and remove from the cardboard.  Make fringe as for shawl.

Lightning Source UK Ltd.
Milton Keynes UK
UKOW051802151211

183864UK00001B/8/P